BUBBLE

TROUBLE

Using mindfulness to help kids with grief

WRITTEN BY
HEATHER KRANTZ, MD

ILLUSTRATED BY
LISA MAY

Bubble Trouble
Published by Herow Press
Bend, Oregon
herowpress.com

ISBN 978-0-9987037-7-0

First printing September, 2018

A Note to Parents, Teachers, and Caregivers:

Grief and loss are difficult concepts for adults let alone children to grasp. The feelings that arise can be confusing and overwhelming. Big changes in a child's life like a move to a new town or the arrival of a new sibling can elicit a grief reaction. When a child experiences the loss of a friend who moves away or a beloved teacher who takes a new job, a child may feel the loss. And certainly the death of a loved one—be it a parent, grandparent, or pet—can leave a child mired in grief. It is our role as parents, teachers, and caregivers to guide children through these difficult changes in life. This isn't always easy, and tools can be helpful.

Mindfulness is one such tool. Mindfulness teaches us to bring awareness to the present moment. We can learn to purposefully redirect our attention from wandering thoughts and feelings back to the breath as a way to anchor ourselves in the present. When children imagine their feelings as bubbles that come and go, they see that difficult emotions change constantly and are not a permanent part of them. It can be a relief to realize that heavy emotions will not last forever.

It is also important for children to learn that feelings resulting from grief are very individual. Each child has a right to feel whatever he or she feels. These feelings can vary across a wide spectrum. Grief can also affect the body causing sleep problems, aches and pains, and appetite changes. Helping to explain and normalize this can ease a child's experience with grief.

Dedicated to my friend Bryn.
And to my illustrator Lisa.

Sometimes feelings can be
so big and confusing.
Do you ever feel like this?

I really love my dog, but he died.
My friend's grandma died too. Another
friend is moving away.

We all feel sad.
We are having big feelings.

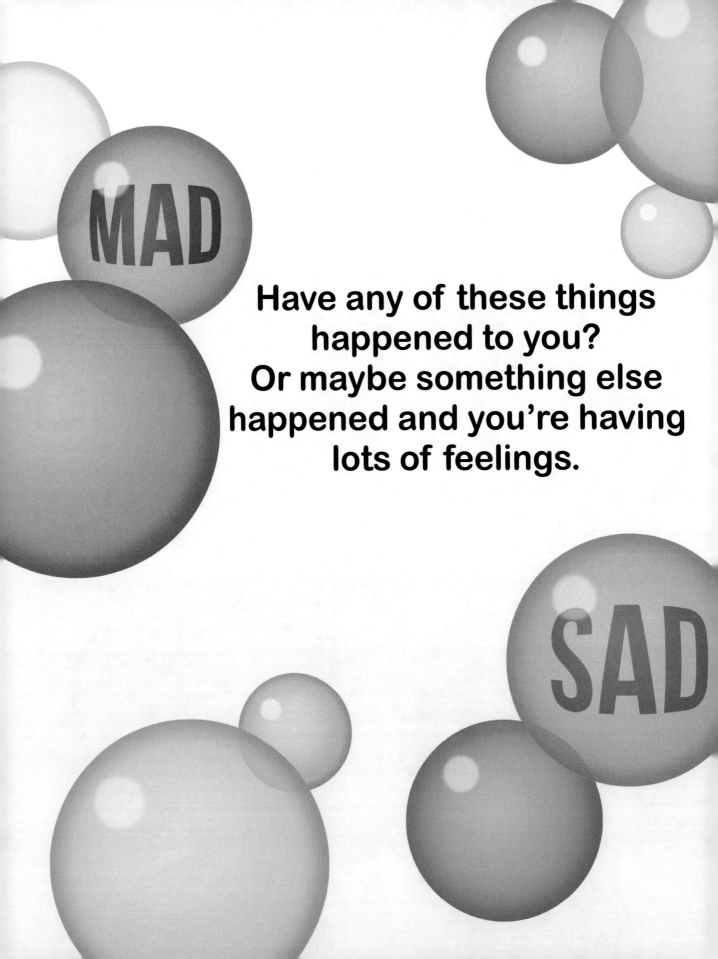

MAD

SAD

Have any of these things happened to you? Or maybe something else happened and you're having lots of feelings.

I'm sad about my dog, but
I also feel a bit relieved.
My dog was very old and sick.
I know he wasn't happy.

My friend says she is sad, but she also feels scared. She misses her grandma, and now she's worried something might happen to someone else she loves.

My other friend says he's sad and also excited about moving.
He will miss his friends, but his new home has a tree house and a bedroom just for him.

How can we all feel sad plus other feelings at the same time?
This is so confusing!

Sometimes feelings just don't
seem to go together.
I feel sad about my dog
and I'm happy that my friend
invited me to her house to play.
I feel sad and happy
at the same time.

I learned from my mom that whenever a difficult change happens it's normal to feel a whole bunch of emotions.

Sometimes my mom uses the word grief to describe this. She says grief shows up in different ways.

I'm feeling grief about my dog.
I can't stop thinking about him
and I cry a lot.

My friend who is moving says he feels nervous and has an upset tummy.

I think my friend is feeling really big grief about her grandma. She can't sleep and doesn't want to eat much.

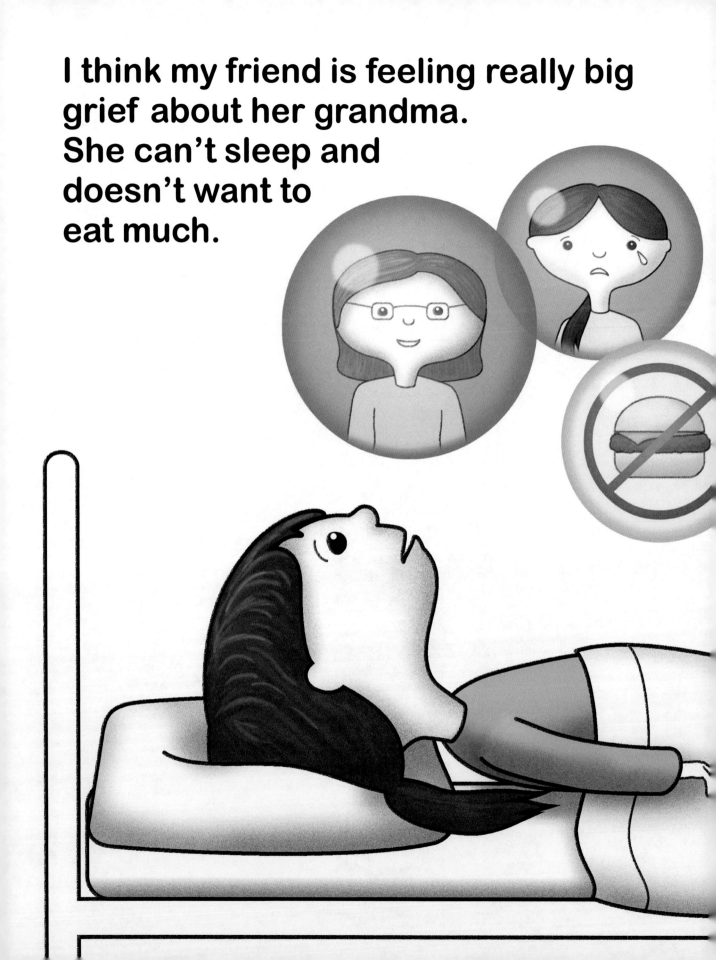

Grief is how we react to a death or a difficult loss or change in life.

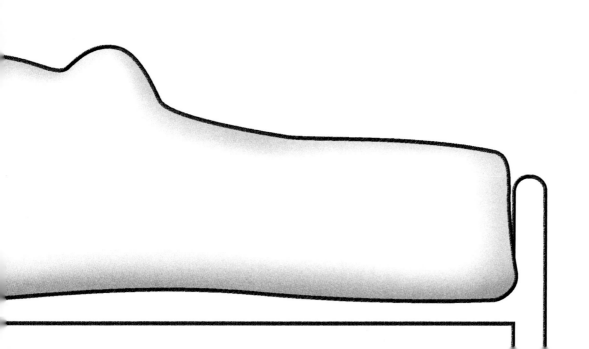

Grief can affect our bodies. It might be hard to sleep, or we might have a headache or tummy ache.

Grief can affect our emotions.
We could feel sad, angry, worried,
afraid, lonely, or confused.
Or maybe all of these things or
something else.

I guess grief is different for each person, and it depends on what happened.

NORMAL

My mom says this is all normal.

But it still can be hard
and hurt a lot.
It's okay to cry.

Sun	Mon	Tues	Wed	Thur	Fri	Sat
			1 ?	2 ?	3 ?	4 ?
5 ?	6 ?	7 ?	8 ?	9 ?	10 ?	11 ?
12 ?	13 ?	14 ?	15 ?	16 ?	17 ?	18
19	20	21	22	23	24	25
26	27	28	29	30		

And how long it lasts just depends.

What can we do about grief?
My mom says the first thing to do is give
yourself a break.

It's okay to feel crummy or sad or whatever you feel.
Don't let anyone tell you to feel differently.

We can also use something called mindfulness to help.
To do this, I pay attention to my breathing and imagine all my thoughts and feelings as bubbles

I notice them float in and out and sometimes pop, but I don't try to make them go away.
I just let them be there.

Difficult bubbles might hang around for awhile, like sadness about my dog.

Sometimes I get out my crayon
and draw some bubbles with
my feelings in them.
It helps.

I notice that the bubbles change over time. Other bubbles show up— like good memories.....

and now I'm not as sad.

I also made a memory box.
I put pictures of my dog and
special things that belonged to him
in a box and decorated it.

Talking with others can help.

I tell my friends
how much I miss my dog.
They talk about their grief too.

Sometimes I just want
to be by myself.
I go outside and look at the clouds
and remember my dog.

I now know that grief happens to all of us and it's okay.

Mindfulness Practice for Grief

(To be read by adult to child.)

Take a few moments to find a comfortable position sitting or lying down and close your eyes.
Put your hand on your belly and breathe in and out.
Feel the rise and fall of your belly.
Breathing in and breathing out.
In and out.
Now imagine yourself wrapped in a warm soft blanket.
Imagine how cozy it feels.
Let your whole body relax and sink into the blanket.

Big changes in life can bring lots of big feelings. This can be scary and confusing.
Let's see if you can imagine those feelings now. See them now as bubbles around you.
Some are big.Some are small. Maybe they are different colors.
All kinds of feelings are in those bubbles.
Sad, mad, scared, lonely.
Maybe happy, relieved, and numb too.
Just notice the bubbles. Let them be there. Notice how some float away,
some change, and some pop.

Now put your hand over your heart.
Tell yourself, "Feelings are like bubbles. They come and go. They aren't a part of me.
I can watch them change."
Feel the warmth of your hand on your chest, and know that all feelings are okay.

Now go back to noticing your breath.
Feeling your breath move gently in and out of your body.
Now gently open your eyes.

Heather Krantz, M.D. is an integrative medicine physician and mindfulness teacher. She is the author of *Mind Bubbles: Exploring mindfulness with kids*, *Heart Bubbles: Exploring compassion with kids*, and *Sleep Bubbles: Using mindfulness to help kids sleep*. She trained as an obstetrician/gynecologist and completed a fellowship in integrative medicine. She now teaches Mindfulness-Based Stress Reduction, Mindful Self-Compassion, and mindfulness workshops and practices mind-body medicine in Bend, Oregon.

Find her at HeatherKrantzMD.com and InSightMindfulnessCenter.com.

Lisa May is a medical illustrator in Sisters, Oregon. She has a Masters of Science in Medical Illustration from the Medical College of Georgia. She has worked for nearly three decades illustrating and designing books, and she has a passion for children's books and reading with kids. She is the illustrator of *Mind Bubbles: Exploring mindfulness with kids*, *Heart Bubbles: Exploring compassion with kids*, and *Sleep Bubbles: Using mindfulness to help kids sleep*.

Find her at LisaMayStudio.com.

Made in the USA
Coppell, TX
02 January 2021